Path to Excellence

Path to Excellence

Building the UNIVERSITY OF OKLAHOMA

1890–2015

Preface by DAVID L. BOREN
Introduction by JOHN R. LOVETT *and* JACQUELYN SLATER REESE
Text by BETHANY R. MOWRY

UNIVERSITY OF OKLAHOMA PRESS : NORMAN
in cooperation with the
UNIVERSITY OF OKLAHOMA FOUNDATION

Front-matter illustrations: p. iii: Bizzell Memorial Library, 2010 (Robert Taylor);
p. vi: portrait of David L. Boren (Robert Taylor); p. viii: *Seed Sower,* by Paul Moore
(Charles Robert Goins); p. 1: North Oval, 1924 (OU Collection 2554a)

ISBN: 978-0-8061-9978-8 (hardcover : alk. paper)

The paper in this book meets the guidelines for permanence and durability of the Committee on Production Guidelines for Book Longevity of the Council on Library Resources, Inc. ∞

1 2 3 4 5 6 7 8 9 10

I looked off to the southwest where

our University was to be located.

There was not a tree or shrub in sight.

All I could see was the monotonous stillness

of prairie grass. . . . Behind me was a crude

little town of 1,500 people and before me

was a stretch of prairie on which my helpers

and I were to build an institution

of culture. Discouraged? Not a bit.

The sight was a challenge.

—DAVID ROSS BOYD

PREFACE

By **DAVID L. BOREN**

UNIVERSITIES ARE REMARKABLE INSTITUTIONS. It has been said that they create more energy than any other institution in our society. It is at the university that the experience and sense of perspective of the older generation collides with the vision, ideals, and hopes of the younger generation. It is at the university where all of the experiences and ideas of those who have come before us are put forward so that we can learn from them. It is at the university where the search for truth is unfettered and the future is shaped.

This book captures in photographs and brief texts, the history of the first 125 years of the University of Oklahoma. We see the institution take root, grow, and develop as the photographs unfold. In the earliest days, the buildings seem so fragile and barely attached to the earth that we are led to wonder if the university will survive. In the end, we see the beauty and strength of one of the greatest public universities in our country.

That evolution didn't happen by chance. It took constant stewardship, sacrifice, and courage. Economic hardship, political neglect, and sometimes political interference and self-doubt had to be overcome. Yet the students, graduates, friends, faculty, and staff of the university maintained the faith of the its first president, David Ross Boyd. Confronted with a barren prairie with no buildings where he was charged with the responsibility of building a university, he wrote in his diary that he saw only great possibilities.

As the University of Oklahoma observes its 125th anniversary, many of those possibilities have been realized. Yet Boyd's words continue to challenge us. This university will never stop reaching for even higher levels of excellence and for more opportunities for our students.

In the past few years, the singing of the alma mater, the OU Chant, has been revitalized. The last words of the chant are both words of determination and words of challenge. The words are "Live On, University." They remind us that great universities like ours live on only if they are loved, supported, and cherished. For the sake of our free society, may it ever be so.

INTRODUCTION

EVERY DAY THE *SEED SOWER* GREETS THOUSANDS OF STUDENTS at the entrance to the South Oval. Sculpted by Artist-in-Residence Paul Moore in the likeness of the first president of the University of Oklahoma, David Ross Boyd, the statue has a plaque affixed to its base commemorating the university's sixtieth anniversary. The first line of the plaque's inscription, written by Professor of History Edward Everett Dale (an OU graduate), reads: THIS IS OUR HERITAGE: THE TRADITIONAL SOONER SPIRIT. Although no one captured on film the moment when President Boyd first laid eyes upon the barren prairie where he would build a university, his vision of a great institution of learning still resonates. Over the past 125 years, "our heritage: the traditional Sooner spirit" has grown to greatness through the contributions of students, faculty, presidents, regents, staff, alumni, and friends of the University of Oklahoma. It is that bond of 125 years that has made and will continue to make this university the great institution of learning that Boyd envisioned.

The same heritage and spirit that inspired Edward Everett Dale's words emerge from the photographs reproduced in this volume. From cover to cover, these images reveal how a single campus with just one building became an institution of higher learning with thriving campuses in three cities and more National Merit Scholars enrolled annually than at any other public university in America. The journey has had its trials, but the OU community's enduring efforts to achieve excellence ensured their alma mater's success.

Path to Excellence would not have been possible without the contributions of President David L. Boren and First Lady Molly Shi Boren. In 1995, President Boren initiated the University Historic Photograph Project, a campuswide endeavor that continues to this day. Designed not just to decorate halls and offices but to provide as well a window on our university's storied past, the Photograph Project directly inspired the creation and composition of this book. President Boren's support and encouragement of the project and of this publication, along with his successful efforts to cultivate true excellence at the university, display the Sooner spirit to the utmost degree. First Lady Molly Shi Boren, whose untiring efforts to make the campuses of the University of Oklahoma true works of beauty, also deserves our thanks for enabling our photographers to capture the university at its very best.

This book was the work of many contributors, both within the university community and in the larger Sooner community. Financial support from the Edward Everett Dale Society of the Western History Collections and the William J. Welch Professorship endowment helped make this project a reality.

We wish to personally thank Professor Emeritus David W. Levy, author of two volumes and counting of *The University of Oklahoma: A History,* for his friendship and encouragement. This book has also been a partnership between the Western History Collections and the University of Oklahoma Press. OU Press Director B. Byron Price and Associate Director and Editor-in-Chief Charles E. Rankin, along with the rest of their exceptional team, have been our guides for this book. Also, OU Press production designer Julie Rushing deserves special credit for her exceptional design work on this book. For all of us, *Path to Excellence* represents our heritage, the traditional Sooner spirit.

JOHN R. LOVETT

Class of 1979

JACQUELYN SLATER REESE

Class of 2009

ACKNOWLEDGMENTS

THIS BOOK WOULD NOT HAVE BEEN POSSIBLE without the efforts and support of people across the university. Special thanks go to our current and former student assistants who provided digitization support all along the way: Elisabeth Branam, Athena Grossman, Christina Hughes, Amy Lantrip, Kathryn Shauberger, and Aaron Votaw. Research conducted by our graduate assistants proved invaluable, so thank you to Hadley Jerman, Bethany Mowry, and Laura Sikes. Our staff assistant, Tara Reynolds, provided many of the photographs and also coordinated efforts between students, graduate assistants, and staff. Special thanks to our Associate Curator, Kristina L. Southwell, for her guidance, support, and expertise throughout this project.

A project of this scope requires collaboration among many divisions of the university. We have been fortunate to work with many departments, some with whom we already had connections and others with whom we were able to form a new link. Thank you to Marty Thompson, former director of the Robert M. Bird Library at the Health Sciences Center; Stewart Brower, Toni Hoberecht, and Nha Huynh of the OU-Tulsa Schusterman Library; Joy Summers-Ables, Director of the Robert M. Bird Library at the Health Sciences Center; Catherine Bishop, Vice President for Public Affairs; Brandy Akbaran of Public Affairs; Tripp Hall, Vice President for Development; Scott Matthews, Jacob Potter, Debbie Copp, Karl Anderson, and Dusty Clements of the Athletics Department; Tracy Kennedy and Aaron Anderson of OU-Tulsa; Jody Foote and Sarah Robbins of University Libraries; Sharon Burchett of the Charles M. Russell Center; Andy Taylor of the Visitor Center; Kelly Stout of Classroom Management; Donna Johnston of the OU Tennis Club; David Mullins, women's tennis head coach; J. R. Caton, Vice President of Operations for the Presbyterian Health Foundation; and Sherry Evans of the President's Office.

As this is a photographic history, the images included and the departments and people who provided them are vital to this project's success. Regarding the historical images reproduced here that come from the Western History Collections, each is credited to the photograph or manuscript collection to which it belongs. Especially for the structures, wings, interiors, gardens, and walks recently built or renovated, we relied heavily on other sources of photographs. Our university-affiliated photography contributors include Robert Taylor and Hugh Scott, university photographers; Tara Reynolds, Western History Collections staff assistant; Kathryn Shauberger, Western History Collections student assistant; Hadley Jerman, Western History Collections graduate assistant; Charles Robert Goins, Professor Emeritus of Regional and City Planning; the OU Health Sciences Center Department of Photography; Jen Tregarthen, Public Relations and Marketing Officer, Sam Noble

Oklahoma Museum of Natural History; Steven Baker, University of Oklahoma Press; and Terry Stover, photographer for OUHSC Photographic Services.

This project also required contributions from several photographers outside the university. Our external photography contributors include ADG Inc., Shane Bevel of Shane Bevel Photography, Ace Cuervo of Ace Cuervo Photography, Lisa Hall of Lisa Hall Photography, David McNeese of McNeese Fitzgerald and Associates, Ty Russell of Ty Russell Photography, John Southern of John Southern Photography, Stacey Don West of Loft Photography, and Shevaun Williams of Shevaun Williams & Associates.

Path to Excellence

FORGING A PATH
and BUILDING A LEGACY

By BETHANY R. MOWRY

B eautiful by day and night, the buildings of the University of Oklahoma testify to the strength of its campus community. Students, faculty, alumni, staff, and OU supporters from all walks of life have left their mark over the past 125 years, joining hearts and minds to create a university whose beauty is matched only by its numerous accomplishments. The journey to the quasquicentennial celebration has not been an easy one, the dizzying highs of academic success tempered by the lows of political and economic crises. This adversity has bolstered the Sooner community's dedication, and its commitment to excellence emanates from every hall of the university.

The University of Oklahoma's first steps on the path to excellence began on December 19, 1890, when the territorial legislature made the dreams of Cleveland County and Oklahoma Territory residents a reality. Their tireless fund-raising and outreach efforts helped the fledgling university acquire the land, buildings, and exceptional academic community it would need to become one of the nation's premier institutions of higher education. Challenges and trials marked the university's early years, but the institution's students and faculty, led by inaugural president David Ross Boyd, met those challenges. Through their perseverance, the modern university took shape, from Science Hall with its numerous laboratories and OU's first Museum of Natural History, to the Carnegie Library, a result of President Boyd's direct plea to steel magnate and philanthropist Andrew Carnegie. University publications soon featured images of a thriving and ever-expanding campus where students and faculty met along shady boulevards and in quiet groves that testified to President Boyd's campaign to bring shade to the prairie.

President Boyd departed the university in 1908, but progress along the path to excellence continued. Boyd leased his Norman home, later named Boyd House, to the university, and this residence housed noted faculty members before it became the well-known residence of successive university presidents. The Administration Building, completed in 1910, replaced the two previous University Hall structures, both destroyed by fire despite the heroic efforts of students, faculty, and staff. Known today as Evans Hall, this building stands as a hallmark of the university's acclaimed Cherokee Gothic architectural style. A new building, later named Jacobson Hall, went through multiple uses before becoming the current Visitor Center and "front door" of the university. By the time this building was constructed, the North Oval—formally named the Parrington Oval in honor of professor, football coach, and oval designer Vernon L. Parrington—linked the university's various buildings into a cohesive unit that continues today as OU's traditional gateway to the public.

When William Bennett Bizzell assumed the university's presidency in February 1925, the campus had already transformed from Boyd's "stretch of prairie" to a burgeoning hub of educational excellence. But greater strides were to come. Even as Bizzell was sworn in as the university's fifth president in the grand auditorium of the new Fine Arts Building, the first on-campus dorms, Hester and Robertson Halls, were taking shape. The Physical Education Building, soon renamed the Field House, would host Sooner athletic programs for decades. Finally, a successful 1922 fund-raising campaign ensured realization of OU's twin dreams of a student union and a stadium whose grand size and scale honored military veterans and reflected Sooner ambitions—and greatness. The Oklahoma Memorial Union and the Oklahoma Memorial Stadium, both dedicated to Sooners who made the ultimate sacrifice during the Great War, were completed in 1929. In that same year, a new library, a long-standing ambition of the university and its president, was completed. The library's stunning architecture would earn it the title Oklahoma's Crown Jewel, and it would be renamed in President Bizzell's honor in 1945.

The next two decades of the university's growth would test the bonds forged in its first forty years, as state and national hardships raged against the redbrick walls of Oklahoma's leading educational institution. Economic depression, war, fluctuating stock markets, and social upheaval: all left their mark on the campus, but faculty, students, and supporters found new and innovative ways to succeed. Savvy administrators garnered the aid of the New Deal's Works Progress Administration at the height of the Great Depression, constructing a building to house ROTC Services in 1936. In future years the WPA building would host the Stovall Museum of Natural History; today, it houses the Henderson-Tolson Cultural Center. When President Franklin D. Roosevelt delivered his "Day of Infamy" speech to the nation, formally declaring the United States' entrance into World War II, OU's students and faculty once more answered the call to arms. Yet even as male and female Sooners left to support the war effort, the U.S. military gave back to OU, establishing the Naval Air Station at North Base in 1942 and the Naval Air Technical Training Center (NATTC), or South Base, used with federal permission during the war and formally purchased by the university in 1961. Servicemen became a common sight on OU's campus as the military prepared men for war service and the university bolstered its enrollment numbers. These wartime partnerships and postwar agreements with the United States Navy vastly increased the number of campus holdings—a welcome addition when the GI Bill had a similar effect on the post-war student population.

During and after the war, private donations remained a reliable source of the university's funding, as alumni and fans gave back to their alma mater on an unprecedented scale. The Van Vleet Oval, more popularly known as the South Oval, developed at a breakneck pace between 1948 and 1958, with the addition of numerous buildings, including Gould and Collings Halls. Old buildings acquired new features and purposes, along with new names that honored professors and generous donors. Hygeia Hall was renamed after the first director of Student Health Services, Dr. Gayfree Ellison, before being transformed from the campus infirmary to the student government space in 1971. The Physics Building, constructed in 1948, changed its name to Nielsen Hall in 1965 to honor retiring professor Jens Rud Nielsen, whom President George Lynn Cross described as "Oklahoma's most distinguished scientist." A new art center, funded in part by Mr. and Mrs. Fred Jones of Oklahoma City in 1971, would bear the name of their son, Fred Jones, Jr., an OU senior who lost his life in a plane crash. OU Regent Lloyd Noble's $1 million gift launched the campaign to finance a new basketball arena, completed in 1975 and named in his honor.

In the 1970s and 1980s, administrators and donors focused on updating and acquiring existing buildings rather than on new construction, safeguarding the university's future amidst a series of national energy crises. Doris W. Neustadt's generous donations supported the 1982 construction of Bizzell Memorial Library's Doris W. Neustadt Wing, which featured the latest in educational technology. The addition also included the E. T. Dunlap Clock Tower, a campus icon now steeped in tradition. As the nation's economic forecast improved in the late 1980s, construction projects planned at the beginning of the decade began to move forward. Catlett Music Center's first phase was completed in 1988, and future phases completed over the next ten years added iconic performance spaces as well as administrative offices and practice spaces. After eight years of construction, the $50 million Sarkeys Energy Center opened in 1990, thanks in part to the generous support of OU alumni and the Sarkeys Foundation through the university's landmark Centennial Campaign.

The University of Oklahoma entered its second century with a legacy built on tradition, innovation, and determination to overcome the greatest of challenges. Buoyed by cautious optimism and a drive to succeed, its next steps on the path to excellence would require strong leadership. The November 1994 arrival of President David L. Boren and First Lady Molly Shi Boren heralded the campus's most recent era of change. Guided by their mentors and by their own experiences on the world stage, the Borens have devoted themselves to restoring OU's past greatness even as they fostered innovations that would gain OU even greater recognition in the new millennium. The result has been a veritable explosion of new buildings and renovations, all thanks to tireless fund-raising efforts and generous donor support.

After one hundred years, time had taken its toll on the university's oldest buildings. Such campus landmarks as the Union and Stadium had been updated through the years, but needed renovation on a scale large enough to preserve their legacy for future Sooners. Other structures, including Hester Hall, needed updates to accommodate new programs such as the College of International Studies. The Boren administration also dedicated itself to the restoration of past traditions, from the clarion call of the Union clock tower's chimes to the renovation of Boyd House, which once again became the official home of the university president. Private donors dedicated their resources to the undertaking and to continued student academic success through scholarship endowments. Old Science Hall, constructed in 1903, received needed renovations befitting its current status as a hub for fine arts and theatre, and was renamed in honor of donor and alumna Beatrice Carr Wallace. McCasland Field House has also received multiple renovations in the past twenty years, providing OU's volleyball, men's gymnastics, and wrestling programs with updated facilities. In 2000, the Western History Collections Reading Room, originally Monnet Hall's Law Library, was restored to its historical glory as a unique space where students, faculty, and staff can research the American West and university history.

The university has also expanded its students' horizons through the use of already-acquired land and the purchase of existing buildings. South Base became the site of OU's Research Campus, where private, public, and academic organizations forge ties amid the National Weather Center, five Partners Place buildings, and other new additions to the university landscape. In 1999 the scattered divisions of OU-Tulsa united on one campus, sold to the university by BP Amoco at a below-market price paid in part from funds provided by the Charles and Lynn Schusterman Family Foundation. Renamed the Schusterman Center, the campus has since seen numerous new additions, including the Diabetes and Cancer Center, the Learning Center, and the Schusterman Library. OU's Health Sciences Center campus in Oklahoma City has seen the addition of clinical and educational buildings, many of which are unified by the Stanton L. Young Walk.

In the new millennium, new construction has appeared across all of OU's campuses, providing modern facilities for faculty and students to both impart and receive exceptional education and health care. Devon Energy, Zarrow, and Price Halls offer new homes for the growing number of OU students preparing for futures in engineering and computer science, social work, and business. Wagner Hall houses the University College, welcoming students who seek tutoring assistance or a quiet place to study. Athletics construction, from new training and competition facilities to updates to existing athletics complexes, ensures that Sooner athletes and fans enjoy the very best conditions for victory on and off the field. Student union additions and updates in Norman, and the construction of the David L. Boren Student Union on the Health Sciences Center campus, provide student services and opportunities for socializing, while new dormitories such as Headington Hall give OU's students and student-athletes new homes-away-from-home. These buildings and others exemplify the Sooner dedication to both tradition and innovation, showcasing advanced technology inside structures carefully designed to harmonize with the university's traditional Cherokee Gothic style.

From its humble prairie origins, the University of Oklahoma has become one of the nation's top public universities, with thriving campuses in three cities and a well-earned reputation for excellence. Today its students reap the benefits of a university whose resources are dedicated to their success, their dreams nurtured through the accomplishments of those pioneers who came before, even as they themselves lay the groundwork for future generations' achievements. With "colors proudly gleaming Red and White," the University of Oklahoma lives on, always moving forward on the path to excellence.

New Administration Building, University of Oklahoma, Norman, Okla.

The third Administration Building, completed 1910
Oklahoma Postcard Collection 2075

Opposite: Detail of Evans Hall (previously Administration Building), renovated 1995–2012
Courtesy of Charles Robert Goins

Evans Hall (1935), PE-ET Elm, planted c. 1906
OU Collection 199

Opposite: Evans Hall, PE-ET Elm Commemorative Plaque, installed 2006
Courtesy of Hadley Jerman

President's Office, Evans Hall, renovated 2000s
Courtesy of Hugh Scott

Opposite: Niche statue of David L. Boren, Evans Hall, installed 1999
Courtesy of Kathryn Shauberger

H. A. and P. X. Johnston Gardens, Evans Hall, installed 1995
Courtesy of Robert Taylor

Visitor Center, Jacobson Hall, renovated 1997
Courtesy of Tara Reynolds

LIBRARY BUILDING, UNIVERSITY OF OKLAHOMA, NORMAN, OKLA.

105563

Library Building, completed 1919
Oklahoma Postcard Collection 2076

Jacobson Hall (previously Library Building), renovated 1997
Courtesy of Robert Taylor

Boyd House, leased 1908
James Shannon Buchanan Collection, Photograph Album, page 2

Boyd House, photographed 2013
Courtesy of Tara Reynolds

Boyd House, renovated 1996
Courtesy of Robert Taylor

Boyd House, renovated 1996
Courtesy of Robert Taylor

Boyd House, photographed December 2004
Courtesy of Robert Taylor

Faculty Club, purchased 1951
Roy E. Heffner Collection P396

Opposite: Charles M. Russell Center for the Study of Art of the American West (previously Faculty Club), renovated 1998–1999
Courtesy of David McNeese

Whitehand Hall, purchased 1946
Roy E. Heffner Collection W1189

Whitehand Hall, renovated 1995
Courtesy of Hugh Scott

Library, University of Oklahoma, Norman, Okla.

Carnegie Building, completed 1903
E. B. Johnson Postcard Collection 32

Carnegie Building, renovated 2012
Courtesy of Hadley Jerman

Monnet Hall, completed 1913
OU Collection 2476

Opposite: Western History Collections Reading Room, Monnet Hall, renovated 2000
Courtesy of Hugh Scott

Beatrice Carr Wallace Old Science Hall (previously University Science Hall), renovated 2009
Courtesy of Robert Taylor

UNIVERSITY SCIENCE HALL, NORMAN, OKLA.

University Science Hall, completed 1903
Oklahoma Postcard Collection 196

Fine Arts Building (later Holmberg Hall), completed 1918
OU Collection 554

Historic Holmberg Hall, Reynolds Performing Arts Center, renovated 2002–2005
Courtesy of Tara Reynolds

Entryway mural, Reynolds Performing Arts Center, completed 2005
Courtesy of Hugh Scott

Opposite: Auditorium, Holmberg Hall, Reynolds Performing Arts Center, renovated 2005
Courtesy of Robert Taylor

Fred Jones Jr. Memorial Art Center (later Fred Jones Jr. Museum of Art), completed 1971
OU EMP 723

Lester Wing, Fred Jones Jr. Museum of Art, added 2005
Courtesy of Robert Taylor

Fred Jones Jr. Art Center, School of Art and Art History, renovated 2005
Courtesy of Robert Taylor

Stuart Wing, Fred Jones Jr. Museum of Art, added 2012
Courtesy of Tara Reynolds

Opposite: Adkins Gallery, Stuart Wing, Fred Jones Jr. Museum of Art, added 2012
Courtesy of Robert Taylor

Catlett Music Center, constructed 1988–1998
Courtesy of Robert Taylor

Opposite: Mildred Andrews Boggess Memorial Organ, Grayce B. Kerr Gothic Hall, Catlett Music Center, installed 1999
Courtesy of Hugh Scott

Oklahoma Memorial Union, completed 1929
Roy E. Heffner Collection P1435

Opposite: Oklahoma Memorial Union, renovated 1995–2004
Courtesy of the Robert Taylor

Beaird Lounge, Oklahoma Memorial Union, renovated 1998
Courtesy of Hadley Jerman

Clarke-Anderson Room, Oklahoma Memorial Union, completed 1998
Courtesy of Hugh Scott

David L. Boren Lounge, Oklahoma Memorial Union, renovated and renamed 2001
Courtesy of Robert Taylor

Will Rogers Room, Oklahoma Memorial Union, renovated 1999
Courtesy of Kathryn Shauberger

Archie W. Dunham–Conoco Student Leadership Center, Oklahoma Memorial Union, completed 2000
Courtesy of Robert Taylor

Conoco Leadership Courtyard, Oklahoma Memorial Union, created 2001
Courtesy of Robert Taylor

Molly Shi Boren Ballroom, Oklahoma Memorial Union, renovated 1998–2004
Courtesy of Robert Taylor

Jan Marie and Richard J. Crawford University Club, Oklahoma Memorial Union, renovated 2013
Courtesy of Robert Taylor

Devon Energy Hall, completed 2010
Courtesy of Robert Taylor

Sarkeys Energy Center, completed 1990
OU Collection 2557

Sarkeys Energy Center, renovated 2010
Courtesy of Robert Taylor

Laurence S. Youngblood Energy Library, Sarkeys Energy Center, renovated 2010
Courtesy of Hugh Scott

Rawl Engineering Practice Facility, completed 2010
Courtesy of Robert Taylor

Lissa and Cy Wagner Hall, completed 2008
Courtesy of the OU Foundation

Wagner Hall living room, completed 2008
Courtesy of Hugh Scott

Price Hall, completed 2005
Courtesy of Robert Taylor

Student lounge, Price Hall, completed 2005
Courtesy of Robert Taylor

LIBRARY, UNIVERSITY OF OKLAHOMA, NORMAN, OKLAHOMA

Bizzell Memorial Library, completed 1929
Oklahoma Postcard Collection 2077

Bizzell Memorial Library, renovated 2014–2015
Courtesy of the OU Foundation

Doris W. Neustadt Wing, Bizzell Memorial Library, added 1982
OU EMP 85388-1

Helmerich Collaborative Learning Center, Bizzell Memorial Library, renovated 2014
Courtesy of Hugh Scott

Gaylord Room, Fifth Floor Special Collections, Bizzell Memorial Library, remodeled 2015
Courtesy of Hugh Scott

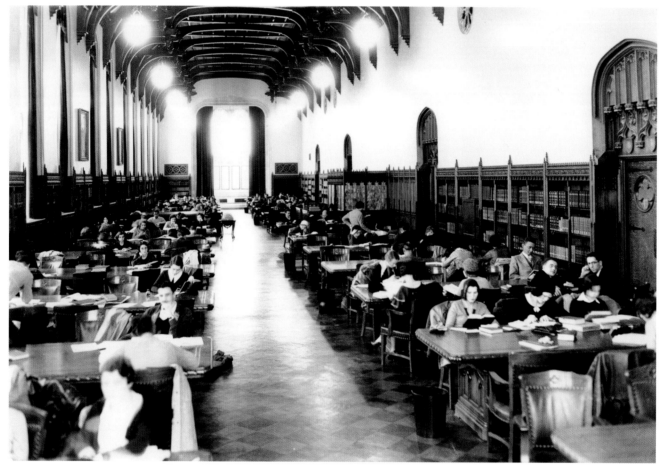

Great Reading Room, Bizzell Memorial Library, completed 1929
William Bennett Bizzell Memorial Library Collection 23

Peggy V. Helmerich Great Reading Room, Bizzell Memorial Library, renovated and renamed 2000

Courtesy of Hugh Scott

Hygeia Hall, completed 1928
OU Collection 1237

Ellison Hall (previously Hygeia Hall), renovated 2000–2003
Courtesy of Robert Taylor

Arts and Sciences Plaza and fountain, Ellison Hall, added 2003
Courtesy of Robert Taylor

Student lounge, Ellison Hall, renovated 2000–2003
Courtesy of Hadley Jerman

Anne and Henry Zarrow Hall of Social Work, completed 2011
Courtesy of Robert Taylor

Courtyard, Zarrow Hall, completed 2011
Courtesy of Robert Taylor

Hester Hall, completed 1926
Roy E. Heffner Collection P8

David L. Boren Lounge, College of International Studies, Hester Hall, renovated 2014
Courtesy of Hugh Scott

Hester Hall, renovated 2014
Courtesy of Hadley Jerman

Classroom, Nielsen Hall, added 2000
Courtesy of Hugh Scott

Physics Building, completed 1948
OU Collection 1640

Nielsen Hall (previously Physics Building), renovated and expanded 2000–2005
Courtesy of Robert Taylor

Gould Hall (School of Geology), completed 1951
OU Collection 1005

Gould Hall (College of Architecture), renovated 2011
Courtesy of Robert Taylor

Buskuhl Gallery, Gould Hall, added 2011
Courtesy of Robert Taylor

Collings Hall, completed 1952
OU Collection 523

Collings Hall, renovated 2010
Courtesy of Tara Reynolds

Gaylord Hall, completed 2004
Courtesy of Robert Taylor

Gaylord Hall expansion, completed 2009
Courtesy of Hugh Scott

Main Lobby, Gaylord Hall, completed 2004
Courtesy of Hugh Scott

Opposite: Ethics and Excellence in Journalism Foundation Auditorium, Gaylord Hall, dedicated 2009
Courtesy of Robert Taylor

David L. Boren Hall, renovated and expanded 1996–2004
Courtesy of Kathryn Shauberger

Wanda Winn Shi Courtyard, David L. Boren Hall, dedicated 2004
Courtesy of Tara Reynolds

Nancy Mergler Library, David L. Boren Hall, dedicated 2006
Courtesy of Tara Reynolds

Law Center, completed 1976
OU EMP 78216–11

Coats Hall (previously Law Center), expanded 2002
Courtesy of the OU Foundation

Donald E. Pray Law Library, Coats Hall, added 2002
Courtesy of the OU Foundation

ROTC Services Building (later home of Stovall Museum of Natural History), completed 1936
Roy E. Heffner Collection V3544

Henderson-Tolson Cultural Center (previously ROTC Services Building), renovated 2002
Courtesy of Kathryn Shauberger

Sam Noble Oklahoma Museum of Natural History, completed 2000
Courtesy of Hadley Jerman

Hall of Natural Wonders, Sam Noble Oklahoma Museum of Natural History, completed 2000
Courtesy of Jen Tregarthen

Traditions Square East, completed 2005
Courtesy of Kathryn Shauberger

Clubhouse, Traditions Square West, completed 2006
Courtesy of Tara Reynolds

David A. Burr Park, dedicated 1996
Courtesy of Tara Reynolds

Stephenson Research and Technology Center, completed 2004
Courtesy of Tara Reynolds

Peggy Stephenson Park, Stephenson Research and Technology Center, dedicated 2011
Courtesy of Kathryn Shauberger

One Partners Place, completed 2004
Courtesy of Kathryn Shauberger

Two Partners Place, completed 2007
Courtesy of Tara Reynolds

Three Partners Place, completed 2009
Courtesy of Kathryn Shauberger

Four Partners Place, completed 2012
Courtesy of Kathryn Shauberger

Five Partners Place, completed 2015
Courtesy of Robert Taylor

National Weather Center, completed 2006
Courtesy of Robert Taylor

Opposite: Atrium with Science on a Sphere display, National Weather Center, completed 2006
Courtesy of Robert Taylor

Stephenson Life Sciences Research Center, completed 2011
Courtesy of Robert Taylor

Seating area, Stephenson Life Sciences Research Center, completed 2011
Courtesy of Robert Taylor

Marita Hynes Field, Softball Complex, completed 1998, renovated 2010
Courtesy of Hugh Scott

John Crain Field, Soccer Complex, completed 2000, renovated 2006
Courtesy of Ty Russell

Gregg Wadley Indoor Tennis Pavilion, completed 2009
Courtesy of Hadley Jerman

Headington Family Tennis Center, completed 2002
Courtesy of Hugh Scott

Lloyd Noble Center, completed 1975
OUCT 2349

Chesapeake Energy Courtside Club, Lloyd Noble Center, added 2001
Courtesy of Robert Taylor

Wick Cary Rowing Training Facility, completed 2015
Courtesy of Hugh Scott

West Dining Hall, Residential Colleges rendering, proposed 2014
Courtesy of ADG Inc. and KWK Architects

Aerial view looking southwest, Residential Colleges rendering, proposed 2014
Courtesy of ADG Inc. and KWK Architects

Headington Hall, completed 2013
Courtesy of Robert Taylor

David and Corty Le Norman Family Q's Commons, Headington Hall, completed 2013
Courtesy of Robert Taylor

Wagner Dining Hall, Headington Hall, completed 2013
Courtesy of Robert Taylor

Field House, completed 1928
OU Collection 1338

McCasland Field House, renovated 2005–2012
Courtesy of Kathryn Shauberger

Asp Avenue Parking Facility, completed 2003
Courtesy of Robert Taylor

Everest Indoor Training Center, completed 2003
Courtesy of Lisa Hall

Oklahoma Memorial Stadium, completed 1929
Emil R. Kraettli Collection 29

Gaylord Family–Oklahoma Memorial Stadium, renovated 2002–2015
Courtesy of the OU Foundation

Sky Suites, Gaylord Family–Oklahoma Memorial Stadium, added 2003
Courtesy of Robert Taylor

Football game at Gaylord Family–Oklahoma Memorial Stadium, renovated 2002–2015
Courtesy of Stacey Don West

South End Zone, Gaylord Family–Oklahoma Memorial Stadium rendering, proposed 2015
Courtesy of OU Athletics Communications

Aerial view, Gaylord Family–Oklahoma Memorial Stadium rendering, proposed 2015
Courtesy of OU Athletics Communications

Stanton L. Young Biomedical Research Center, Health Sciences Center, completed 1997, expanded 2005
Courtesy of Tara Reynolds

OU Physicians, Health Sciences Center, completed 2001
Courtesy of Tara Reynolds

Stanton L. Young Walk, Health Sciences Center, completed 2002
Courtesy of Tara Reynolds

David L. Boren Student Union, Health Sciences Center, completed 2004
Courtesy of OU Health Sciences Center Department of Photography

Student lounge, David L. Boren Student Union, Health Sciences Center, completed 2004
Courtesy of Tara Reynolds

Harold Hamm Oklahoma Diabetes Center, Health Sciences Center, purchased 2008, renovated 2010

Courtesy of Robert Taylor

College of Allied Health, Health Sciences Center, completed 2009
Courtesy of Tara Reynolds

Lobby of College of Allied Health, Health Sciences Center, completed 2009
Courtesy of Tara Reynolds

Children's Hospital, Health Sciences Center, completed 2009
Courtesy of Steven Baker

Atrium, Children's Hospital, Health Sciences Center, completed 2009
Courtesy of University Public Affairs

Stephenson Cancer Center, Health Sciences Center, completed 2011
Courtesy of Robert Taylor

Peggy Stephenson Healing Garden, Stephenson Cancer Center, completed 2011
Courtesy of Robert Taylor

Healthy Hearth, Stephenson Cancer Center, completed 2011
Courtesy of Robert Taylor

University Research Park, Health Sciences Center, acquired 2015
Courtesy of the Presbyterian Health Foundation

OU-Tulsa Schusterman Center, aerial view, photographed 2011
Courtesy of John Southern

Opposite: Schusterman Center Clinic, OU-Tulsa Schusterman Center, completed 2007
Courtesy of Shane Bevel

Founders Hall, Learning Center, OU-Tulsa Schusterman Center, completed 2008
Courtesy of Shane Bevel

Perkins Family Auditorium, Learning Center, OU-Tulsa Schusterman Center, completed 2008
Courtesy of Shane Bevel

Opposite: Learning Center, OU-Tulsa Schusterman Center, completed 2008
Courtesy of Shane Bevel

Diabetes and Cancer Center, OU-Tulsa Schusterman Center, completed 2009
Courtesy of Shane Bevel

Schusterman Library, OU-Tulsa Schusterman Center, completed 2011
Courtesy of Shane Bevel

Wayman Tisdale Specialty Health Clinic, OU-Tulsa, completed 2013
Courtesy of Shane Bevel

CAMPUS BEAUTIFUL
BY DAY *and* NIGHT

K nown for the crimson-and-cream Cherokee Gothic architecture that stands amid lush green landscapes, the University of Oklahoma is one of the state's crown jewels—and its splendor is a point of pride for students, faculty, and staff. Named one of America's most beautiful college campuses in 2014, the university features stately buildings whose fine architectural details are enhanced by manicured lawns and colorful seasonal flowerbeds. Garden spaces and seating areas across the campus provide members of the university community with opportunities for fresh air and outdoor activities, enhancing the college experience. Unique campus highlights such as teak benches, red telephone booths, and sculptures by famous artists showcase the distinctive character of a university nationally recognized for its excellence. Rain or shine, day or night, and in any season, there is always something beautiful to see at the University of Oklahoma.

Scholars Walk, established 2014
Courtesy of Robert Taylor

Anne and Henry Zarrow Hall
Courtesy of Robert Taylor

Price Hall Courtyard
Courtesy of Shevaun Williams

Evans Hall
Courtesy of Robert Taylor

Gould Hall
Courtesy of Robert Taylor

Teak benches near Gould Hall
Courtesy of Charles Robert Goins

LOVE sculpture (by Robert Indiana)
at Jacobson Hall
Courtesy of Tara Reynolds

Gaylord Hall
Courtesy of Robert Taylor

Amish Gazebo at Burr Park
Courtesy of Robert Taylor

May We Have Peace (by Allan Houser)
in Parrington Oval
Courtesy of Robert Taylor

Wagner Hall
Courtesy of Robert Taylor

College of Allied Health, Health Sciences Center
Courtesy of Terry Stover

Bizzell Memorial Library
Courtesy of Hugh Scott

Atrium of Schusterman Center Clinic, OU-Tulsa Schusterman Center
Courtesy of Ace Cuervo

Stuart Art Walk
Courtesy of McNeese Fitzgerald Associates

Jeannine Rainbolt College of Education, Collings Hall
Courtesy of Charles Robert Goins